GEORGE
W
Bushisms

The *Slate* Book of the Accidental Wit and Wisdom of Our Forty-third President

EDITED BY JACOB WEISBERG

FIRESIDE

New York London Toronto Sydney Singapore

FIRESIDE
Rockefeller Center
1230 Avenue of the Americas
New York, NY 10020

FIRESIDE and colophon are registered trademarks
of Simon & Schuster, Inc.

Designed by Bonni Leon-Berman

Manufactured in the United States of America

19   20

Library of Congress Cataloging-in-Publication Data is
available.

ISBN 0-7432-2222-9

Photo credits appear on page 96.

INTRODUCTION

Collecting these utterances by our now president over the past year and a bit, I've found myself returning time and again to the same question: What exactly is wrong with this guy?

The most widely publicized clinical evaluation came from Gail Sheehy, the famed psycho-journalist. Sheehy wrote a lengthy article in *Vanity Fair* proposing that George W. Bush suffers from undiagnosed dyslexia. Within a few hours of the piece's publication, the Republican nominee had responded, "The woman who knew that I had dyslexia—I never interviewed her." People who read this quote in the newspaper might have thought the Texas governor was kidding around. Reporters like me who were surrounding him on an airport tarmac in California when he made the remark knew that, alas, he was not trying to be funny.

That comment notwithstanding, I don't think Bush is dyslexic. When confronted with a TelePrompTer, Bush squints, knits his eyebrows, and peers into it like an admiral trying to discern landfall in the twilight. Yet he has no special trouble rendering his speechwriter's words in the proper order as they scroll past his eyeballs. The trouble arises when Bush isn't reading what someone else has written for him, and comes up with stuff like "I understand small business growth. I was one" or "What a good man the Englers are!"

Dana Milbank of *The Washington Post* identified another possible pathology. Bush, Milbank suggested, might have contracted a mild case of apraxia. According to Lyn Goldberg, a speech pathologist at George Washington University, victims of apraxia have trouble selecting, timing and ordering sounds, which causes them to shorten words (as in "vile" for "viable" or "subsidiation" for "subsidization"). But this can't be it either. Bush just as often reinterprets familiar words by making them longer (as in "subliminable" or "analyzation"). And apraxia, which is often caused by a stroke, is a serious disorder that disrupts neural programming and often leaves its patients unable to speak at all. Bush has not been afflicted to this degree, though at times he does appear headed in that direction.

Could the Man from Midland simply be a bit thick? Texas troublemakers like Paul Begala and Molly Ivins tend to favor this view, expressing it in the sort of colorful metaphor for which their state is known. Our president ain't the brightest bulb on the tree. He ain't the sharpest tool in the shed, either. He may be a few fries short of a Happy Meal, etc., etc. Some of Bush's comments do lend support to this interpretation. I'm thinking of Bush's accusation that Democrats treat

Social Security "like it's some kind of federal program," and the postelection civics lesson in which he reminded us, "The legislature's job is to write law. It's the executive branch's job to interpret law." Under the educational standards Bush has supported in Texas, he'd be doing eighth grade for the thirty-ninth time. Still, I think we have to admit that Dubya is no Dan Quayle. In fact, he's much funnier.

My own hunch is that there's a hereditary component to this trouble. George W. Bush's father George H. W. Bush wasn't dumb, but he sits beside Eisenhower and Coolidge in our pantheon of verbally challenged presidents. When Bush I extemporized, he would dispense with pronouns and verbs ("message: I care"), temper any expression of feeling with words like "stuff" and "thing" ("the vision thing") and often break in mid-thought to accept another incoming mental message, a tendency my friend Tim Noah dubbed his "call-waiting mode." No reporter present that day in New Hampshire will ever forget H.W.'s great reelection riff: "Remember Lincoln, going to his knees in times of trial and the Civil War and all that stuff. You can't be. And we are blessed. So don't feel sorry for—don't cry for me, Argentina. We've got problems out there and I am blessed by good health, strong health. Jeez, you get the flu, and they make it into a federal case. Anyway, that goes with the territory." It was words like these that first provoked me to coin the term "Bushism" a decade ago, on the model of the "Reaganism of the Week" that used to appear in Lou Cannon's column in *The Washington Post*.

Could there be some defect in the Bush language genes? In his book *The Language Instinct*, Stephen Pinker of MIT describes a study done by a linguist named Myrna Gopnik about a group of subjects she calls Family K. While otherwise normally literate and intelligent, the Ks cannot make their subjects and verbs agree in number. "The boys eat four cookie," one will say. "Is our children learning?" another will ask. Professor Gopnik refers to this inherited problem as specific language impairment," or SLI. When I came across this passage in Pinker's book, I thought I'd made a great discovery. The Bushes were Family K!

In fairness, though, George the father doesn't suffer from subject-verb agreement difficulties. And George the son has some language gaps apparently unrelated to SLI. They are, to name just a few, Archie Bunkeresque malapropisms ("I am a person who recognizes the fallacy of humans"); spoonerisms ("terriers and barriffs"); positive-negative confusions ("If I'm president . . . we're going to have gag orders"); truisms ("I think we agree, the past is over"); redundancies ("finality has finally happened"); familiar expressions, often dealing with eating, blackjacked and rendered senseless ("make the pie higher," "put food on your family"); not to mention moments of sheer goofball exuberance that rival Dad's finest ("I know the human being and fish can coexist peacefully").

While the possibility that someone will positively identify the president's pathology remains open, I've become skeptical about finding a single key. My current explanation draws on the nature and the culture of the Bushes. You start with the father tongue, the Cliffs Notes version of *The Preppie Handbook*. Marinate it in the refinery haze of Midland, Texas. Then return east for one of the fanciest and least effective educations ever attempted. Stir briskly and release under pressure. What you get are the gems of accidental wit that follow. For many of them I have to thank the readers of Slate.com, who contributed voluminously during the course of the campaign, as well the boys and girls on the Bush bus. You know who you are.

In lieu of a more accurate diagnosis, enjoy.

—*Jacob Weisberg*

GEORGE
W
Bushisms

WHAT I STAND FOR I

"If you're sick and tired of the politics of cynicism and polls and principles, come and join this campaign."

—*Hilton Head, South Carolina, February 16, 2000*

READY OR NOT

"I don't know whether I'm going to win or not. I think I am. I do know I'm ready for the job. And if not, that's just the way it goes."

—*Des Moines, Iowa, August 21, 2000*

WHAT I STAND FOR II

"This is Preservation Month. I appreciate preservation. It's what you do when you run for president. You gotta preserve."

—*Speaking during Perseverance Month at Fairgrounds Elementary School in Nashua, New Hampshire. Quoted in the* Los Angeles Times, *January 28, 2000*

SMALL BUSINESS

**"I understand small business growth.
I was one."**

—*New York* Daily News, *February 19, 2000*

LEADERSHIP

"I have a different vision of leadership. A leadership is someone who brings people together."

—Bartlett, Tennessee, August 18, 2000

HUMAN NATURE

"I am a person who recognizes the fallacy of humans."

—Oprah, *September 19, 2000*

CATCH AND RELEASE

"I know the human being and fish can coexist peacefully."

—*Saginaw, Michigan, September 29, 2000*

OIL AND WATER

"It is clear our nation is reliant upon big foreign oil. More and more of our imports come from overseas."

—*Beaverton, Oregon, September 25, 2000*

THE RESPONSIBILITY ERA

"I want each and every American to know for certain that I'm responsible for the decisions I make, and each of you are as well."

—Live with Regis, *September 20, 2000*

CLEAN SHEETS

"The administration I'll bring is
a group of men and women who are
focused on what's best for America,
honest men and women, decent men
and women, women who will see
service to our country as a great
privilege and who will not
stain the house."

—*Des Moines, Iowa, January 15, 2000*

UNDERCOUNT

**"They have miscalculated
me as a leader."**

—Westminster, California, September 13, 2000

"They misunderestimated me."

—Bentonville, Arkansas, November 6, 2000

RESIGNED TO LEAD

"They said, 'You know, this issue doesn't seem to resignate with the people.' And I said, 'You know something? Whether it resignates or not doesn't matter to me, because I stand for doing what's the right thing, and what the right thing is hearing the voices of people who work.'"

—*Portland, Oregon, October 31, 2000*

OVERHEARD

"I regret that a private comment I made to the vice presidential candidate made it through the public airways."

—Allentown, Pennsylvania, September 5, 2000

THE NEW CENTURION

"That's a chapter, the last chapter
of the twentieth, twentieth,
twenty-first century that most
of us would rather forget.
The last chapter of the
twentieth century.
This is the first chapter of
the twenty-first century."

—Arlington Heights, Illinois, October 24, 2000

CONVICTION

"I think if you know what you believe, it makes it a lot easier to answer questions. I can't answer your question."

—*Reynoldsburg, Ohio, October 4, 2000*

TRUST

"There's a huge trust. I see it all the time when people come up to me and say, 'I don't want you to let me down again.'"

—*Boston, Massachusetts, October 3, 2000*

"Well, I think if you say you're going to do something and don't do it, that's trustworthiness."

—*CNN online chat, August 30, 2000*

MR. BUSH'S NEIGHBORHOOD

"We must all hear the universal call to like your neighbor just like you like to be liked yourself."

—Financial Times, *January 14, 2000*

TIME

"The best way to relieve families from time is to let them keep some of their own money."

—*Westminster, California, September 13, 2000*

FAITH

"Our priorities is our faith."

—*Greensboro, North Carolina, October 10, 2000*

"We have practically banished
religious values and religious institutions
from the public square and constructed a
'discountfort zone' for even discussing our
faith in public settings."

—*Milwaukee, Wisconsin, September 9, 2000*

FAMILY

"Families is where our nation finds hope, where wings take dream."

—La Crosse, Wisconsin, October 18, 2000

ESPECIALLY WHEN THEY WON'T HOLD STILL

"I know how hard it is for you to put food on your family."

—*Nashua, New Hampshire,*
January 27, 2000

GIST FOR THE MILL

**"I thought how proud I am to be
standing up beside my dad.
Never did it occur to me that he
would become the
gist for cartoonists."**

—Newsweek, *February 28, 2000*

SHIRT STUD

"We want our teachers to be trained so they can meet the obligations, their obligations as teachers. We want them to know how to teach the science of reading. In order to make sure there's not this kind of federal—federal cufflink."

—*Fritsche Middle School, Milwaukee, Wisconsin, March 30, 2000*

READING

"Reading is the basics for all learning."

—Reston, Virginia, March 28, 2000

**"One of the great things about
books is sometimes there are some
fantastic pictures."**

—U.S. News & World Report, January 3, 2000

PERHAPS NOT

**"Rarely is the question asked:
Is our children learning?"**

—*Florence, South Carolina,
January 11, 2000*

THE PARENTS IS LEARNING

"Laura and I really don't realize how bright our children is sometimes until we get an objective analysis."

—Meet the Press, *April 15, 2000*

CURIOUS GEORGE

"It's clearly a budget. It's got a lot of numbers in it."

—Reuters, May 5, 2000

BUT I COULD IF I WANTED TO

"I don't read what's handed to me."

> —The New York Times,
> *March 15, 2000*

"The woman who knew that I had dyslexia—I never interviewed her."

> —*Orange, California, September 15, 2000*

PASS

"As governor of Texas, I have set high standards for our public schools, and I have met those standards."

—CNN online chat, August 30, 2000

A TERRIBLE THING TO WASTE

"How do you know if you don't measure if you have a system that simply suckles kids through?"

—*Explaining the need for educational accountability in Beaufort, South Carolina, February 16, 2000*

"Governor Bush will not stand for the subsidation of failure."

—*Florence, South Carolina, January 11, 2000*

IS THE CONDOMS WORKING?

"I think it's important for those of us in a position of responsibility to be firm in sharing our experiences, to understand that the babies out of wedlock is a very difficult chore for mom and baby alike. . . . I believe we ought to say there is a different alternative than the culture that is proposed by people like Miss Wolf in society. . . . And, you know, hopefully, condoms will work, but it hasn't worked."

—Meet the Press, *November 21, 1999*

THE HEARTBEAT OF AMERICA

"We'll let our friends be the peacekeepers and the great country called America will be the pacemakers."

—*Houston, Texas, September 6, 2000*

SKEPTICISM

"The fundamental question is,
'Will I be a successful president when
it comes to foreign policy?' I will be,
but until I'm the president, it's going to
be hard for me to verify that I think
I'll be more effective."

—*Wayne, Michigan, June 27, 2000*

CALLING CONDE I

"I hope to get a sense of,
should I be fortunate enough to be
the president, how my administration
will react to the Middle East."

—*Winston-Salem, North Carolina,*
October 12, 2000

CALLING CONDE II

"If the East Timorians decide to revolt, I'm sure I'll have a statement."

—The New York Times, *June 16, 1999*

"Kosovians can move back in."

—CNN Inside Politics, *April 9, 1999*

"The only thing I know about Slovakia is what I learned firsthand from your foreign minister, who came to Texas."

—*To a Slovak journalist, as quoted by Knight Ridder News Service, June 22, 1999. Bush's meeting was with Janez Drnovsek, the prime minister of Slovenia.*

GRECIAN FORMULA

"Keep good relations with the Grecians."

—The Economist, *June 12, 1999*

FOREIGN POLICY

"I will have a foreign-handed foreign policy."

—Redwood, California, September 27, 2000

"We cannot let terrorists and rogue nations hold this nation hostile or hold our allies hostile."

—Des Moines, Iowa, August 21, 2000

DANGEROUS WORLD

"When I was coming up, it was a
dangerous world, and you knew exactly
who they were. It was us versus them, and
it was clear who them was.
Today we are not so sure who the they are,
but we know they're there."

—*Iowa Western Community College,*
January 21, 2000

"This is still a dangerous world.
It's a world of madmen and uncertainty
and potential menshul losses."

—Financial Times, *January 14, 2000*

MISCEGENATION

"The Bob Jones policy on interracial dating, I mean I spoke out on interracial dating. I spoke out against that. I spoke out against interracial dating. I support the policy of interracial dating."

—CBS News, February 25, 2000

YOUNG GUNS

"I think we ought to raise the age at which juveniles can have a gun."

—*St. Louis, Missouri, October 18, 2000*

NO VACANCY

"I don't have to accept their tenants.
I was trying to convince those college
students to accept my tenants.
And I reject any labeling me because
I happened to go to the university."

—Today, *February 23, 2000*

BALKANIZATION

"What I am against is quotas.
I am against hard quotas, quotas they
basically delineate based upon whatever.
However they delineate, quotas, I think
vulcanize society. So I don't know how that
fits into what everybody else is saying, their
relative positions, but that's my position."

—San Francisco Chronicle,
January 21, 2000

THE AMERICAN WAY

"Quotas are bad for America.
It's not the way America is all about."

—*St. Louis, Missouri, October 18, 2000*

"If affirmative action means what I just
described, what I'm for, then I'm for it."

—*St. Louis, Missouri, October 18, 2000*

ARRESTED FOR DRIVING
WHILE READING

"I mean, there needs to be a
wholesale effort against racial profiling,
which is illiterate children."

—*Winston-Salem, North Carolina, October 11, 2000*

DUNGEONS AND DRAGONS

"It's important for us to explain to our nation that life is important. It's not only life of babies, but it's life of children living in, you know, the dark dungeons of the Internet."

—*Arlington Heights, Illinois, October 24, 2000*

INFOJAM

"Will the highways on the Internet become more few?"

—*Concord, New Hampshire, January 29, 2000*

LIFE

"States should have the right
to enact reasonable laws and
restrictions particularly to end the
inhumane practice of ending a life
that otherwise could live."

—*Cleveland, Ohio, June 29, 2000*

DEATH

"The only things that I can tell you is
that every case I have reviewed I have
been comfortable with the innocence or
guilt of the person that I've looked at.
I do not believe we've put a guilty—
I mean, innocent person to death
in the state of Texas."

—*National Public Radio, June 16, 2000*

"This case has had full analyzation and
has been looked at a lot. I understand the
emotionality of death penalty cases."

—*Seattle Post-Intelligencer, June 23, 2000*

DEATH AND TAXES I

"Mr. Vice President, in all due respect,
it is—I'm not sure 80 percent of the people
get the death tax. I know this: 100 percent
will get it if I'm the president."

—*St. Louis, Missouri, October 18, 2000*

DEATH AND TAXES II

"It's going to require numerous IRA agents."

—*On Gore's tax plan, Greensboro, North Carolina, October 10, 2000*

EVER HEAR THE ONE ABOUT THE SICK ECONOMY?

"A tax cut is really one of the anecdotes to coming out of an economic illness."

—The Edge with Paula Zahn, *September 18, 2000*

MY PREDECESSORS

"It is not Reaganesque to support a tax plan that is Clinton in nature."

—Los Angeles, February 23, 2000

MONEY

"The government is not the surplus's money, Vice President."

—The Washington Post, *November 5, 2000*

"It's your money. You paid for it."

—*La Crosse, Wisconsin, October 18, 2000*

WOOF

"If the terriers and bariffs are torn down, this economy will grow."

—*Rochester, New York, January 7, 2000*

HELP WANTED

"Dick Cheney and I do not
want this nation to be in a recession.
We want anybody who can find work to
be able to find work."

—60 Minutes II, *December 5, 2000*

THE PHANTOM
TOLLBOOTH

"I think we need not only to eliminate the tollbooth to the middle class, I think we should knock down the tollbooth."

—*Nashua, New Hampshire, as quoted in* The New York Times, *February 1, 2000*

OVERHEAD SLICE

"We ought to make the pie higher."

—Columbia, South Carolina,
February 15, 2000

INSECURITY

"There's not going to be enough people in the system to take advantage of people like me."

—*On the coming Social Security crisis,*
Wilton, Connecticut, June 9, 2000

"They want the federal government controlling Social Security like it's some kind of federal program."

—*St. Charles, Missouri, November 2, 2000*

JUDGE NOT

"The legislature's job is to write law.
It's the executive branch's job to
interpret law."

—*Austin, Texas, November 22, 2000*

GREAT EXPECTATIONS

**"One of the common denominators
I have found is that expectations rise
above that which is expected."**

—*Los Angeles, September 27, 2000*

THINK FIRST

"I want you to know that farmers are not going to be secondary thoughts to a Bush administration. They will be in the forethought of our thinking."

—*Salinas, California, August 10, 2000*

"This campaign not only hears the voices of the entrepreneurs and the farmers and the entrepreneurs, we hear the voices of those struggling to get ahead."

—*Des Moines, Iowa, August 21, 2000*

LOOKING BACK

"I think we agree, the past is over."

—*On his meeting with John McCain,*
The Dallas Morning News, *May 10, 2000*

THE BOTTOM

"I hope we get to the bottom of the answer. It's what I'm interested to know."

—Associated Press, April 26, 2000

CHALLENGED

"Listen, Al Gore is a very tough opponent. He is the incumbent. He represents the incumbency. And a challenger is somebody who generally comes from the pack and wins, if you're going to win. And that's where I'm coming from."

—*Detroit, September 7, 2000*

RUDY

**"He has certainly earned a
reputation as a fantastic mayor,
because the results speak for themselves.
I mean, New York's a safer place for
him to be."**

—*On Rudy Giuliani,* The Edge with Paula Zahn,
May 18, 2000

JOHN

"The senator has got to understand if he's going to have—he can't have it both ways. He can't take the high horse and then claim the low road."

—Florence, South Carolina,
February 17, 2000

DICK

TED KOPPEL: So he's your lightning rod?

BUSH: More than that, he's my sounding rod.

—On Vice President Cheney, Nightline,
July 21, 2000

AL

"The fact that he relies on facts—says things that are not factual—are going to undermine his campaign."

—The New York Times, *March 4, 2000*

JEB

GOVERNOR BUSH: I talked to my little brother, Jeb—I haven't told this to many people. But he's the governor of—I shouldn't call him my little brother—my brother, Jeb, the great governor of Texas.

JIM LEHRER: Florida.

GOVERNOR BUSH: Florida. The state of the Florida.

—The NewsHour with Jim Lehrer, *April 27, 2000*

GEORGE

"Actually, I—this may sound a little
West Texan to you, but I like it. When
I'm talking about—when I'm talking about
myself, and when he's talking about myself,
all of us are talking about me."

—Hardball, *May 31, 2000*

LAURA

"The most important job is not to
be governor, or first lady in my case."

—*Pella, Iowa, quoted in the* San Antonio Express-News,
January 30, 2000

THE ENGLER

"Laura and I are proud to call John and Michelle Engler our friends. I know you're proud to call him governor. What a good man the Englers are."

—*Grand Rapids, Michigan, November 3, 2000*

TOUGH CHOICE

"It's evolutionary, going from governor
to president, and this is a significant step,
to be able to vote for yourself on the ballot,
and I'll be able to do so next fall, I hope."

—*Associated Press, March 8, 2000*

CAMPAIGN

**"The important question is,
how many hands have I shaked?"**

—The New York Times, *October 23, 1999*

**"I don't want to win? If that were the
case, why the heck am I on the bus sixteen
hours a day, shaking thousands of hands,
giving hundreds of speeches, getting
pillared in the press and cartoons and
still staying on message to win?"**

—Newsweek, *February 28, 2000*

GRATITUDE

"Really proud of it. A great campaign.
And I'm really pleased with the organization
and the thousands of South Carolinians
that worked on my behalf. And I'm
very gracious and humbled."

—This Week, *February 20, 2000*

PERIODICALS

"I do not agree with this notion that somehow if I go to try to attract votes and to lead people toward a better tomorrow somehow I get subscribed to some—some doctrine gets subscribed to me."

—Meet the Press, *February 13, 2000*

ON STYLE

"I've changed my style somewhat,
as you know. I'm less—I pontificate less,
although it may be hard to tell it from
this show. And I'm more interacting
with people."

—Meet the Press, *February 13, 2000*

ON DRUGS

"Drug therapies are replacing a lot of medicines as we used to know it."

—St. Louis, Missouri, October 18, 2000

ON MESSAGE

"I don't think we need to be subliminable about the differences between our views on prescription drugs."

—Orlando, Florida, September 12, 2000

QUIET IN THE ER

"If I'm the president, we're going to have emergency-room care, we're going to have gag orders."

—*St. Louis, Missouri, October 18, 2000*

"It's one thing about insurance, that's a Washington term."

—*St. Louis, Missouri, October 18, 2000*

DUCK AND UNCOVER

"That's Washington.
That's the place where you find
people getting ready to jump out of the
foxholes before the first shot is fired."

—*Westland, Michigan, September 8, 2000*

GEOGRAPHY

"I was raised in the West.
The west of Texas. It's pretty close
to California. In more ways than
Washington, D.C., is close
to California."

—*Los Angeles, April 7, 2000*

ESPECIALLY AFTER
EIGHT OR TEN BEERS

**"It was just inebriating what Midland
was all about then."**

—From a 1994 interview, as quoted in
First Son *by Bill Minutaglio*

METAPHYSICS

"I'm gonna talk about the ideal world,
Chris. I've read—I understand reality.
If you're asking me as the president,
would I understand reality, I do."

—Hardball, *May 31, 2000*

DELEGATION

"As far as the legal hassling and
wrangling and posturing in Florida,
I would suggest you talk to our team
in Florida led by Jim Baker."

—*Crawford, Texas, November 30, 2000*

THE NOMINEE
PRESUMPTUOUS

"It is incredibly presumptive for somebody who has not yet earned his party's nomination to start speculating about vice presidents."

—Keene, New Hampshire, October 22, 1999

GOOD ENOUGH

"What I'm suggesting to you is,
if you can't name the foreign minister
of Mexico, therefore, you know, you're
not capable of what you do. But the truth
of the matter is you are, whether you can
or not."

—Seattle Post-Intelligencer,
November 6, 1999

SMART ENOUGH

"There is book smart and the kind of smart that helps do calculus. But smart is also instinct and judgment and common sense. Smart comes in all kinds of different ways."

—*CNN, September 19, 2000*

"I think anybody who doesn't think I'm smart enough to handle the job is underestimating."

—U.S. News & World Report, *April 3, 2000*

AND DOGGONE IT,
PEOPLE LIKE ME

"This is what I'm good at.
I like meeting people, my fellow citizens,
I like interfacing with them."

—*Outside Pittsburgh, September 8, 2000*

IN CONCLUSION

**"I knew it might put him in an
awkward position that we had a
discussion before finality has finally
happened in this presidential race."**

*—Describing a phone call to Senator John Breaux,
Crawford, Texas, December 2, 2000*

Photo Credits

AP/Wide World Photos: title page photo, 31, 37, 65

Reuters New Media/Corbis: running head photo, 20, 35, 43, 54, 62, 72, 81, 91

AFP/Corbis: 15, 33, 53, 94, 95

Reuters New Media/Corbis: 16, 58, 68, 92, 37

AFP/Corbis: 18, 25, 36, 63, 70, 71, 89

Reuters New Media/Corbis: 19, 37, 46, 56, 78, 79, 88

AP/Wide World Photos: 22, 24, 32, 49, 67, 87

Reuters New Media/Corbis: 26, 30, 37, 44, 60, 73, 82

AP/Wide World Photos: 39, 51, 90

AP/Wide World Photos: 42, 50, 74, 86